The Chatter that Matters

The Chatter that Matters

Your Words *ARE* Your Power

Margaret Martin

"A man is literally what he thinks, his character being the complete sum of all of his thoughts."

. . . *James Allen*

BALBOA.
PRESS

A DIVISION OF HAY HOUSE

ISBN: 978-1-4525-5208-8 (sc)
ISBN: 978-1-4525-5209-5 (hc)
ISBN: 978-1-4525-5207-1 (e)

Library of Congress Control Number: 2012908045

Balboa Press books may be ordered through booksellers or by contacting:
Balboa Press
A Division of Hay House
1663 Liberty Drive
Bloomington, IN 47403
www.balboapress.com
1-(877) 407-4847

Because of the dynamic nature of the Internet, any web addresses or links contained in this book may have changed since publication and may no longer be valid. The views expressed in this work are solely those of the author and do not necessarily reflect the views of the publisher, and the publisher hereby disclaims any responsibility for them.

The author of this book does not dispense medical advice or prescribe the use of any technique as a form of treatment for physical, emotional, or medical problems without the advice of a physician, either directly or indirectly. The intent of the author is only to offer information of a general nature to help you in your quest for emotional and spiritual well-being. In the event you use any of the information in this book for yourself, which is your constitutional right, the author and the publisher assume no responsibility for your actions.

Any people depicted in stock imagery provided by Thinkstock are models, and such images are being used for illustrative purposes only.
Certain stock imagery © Thinkstock.

Printed in the United States of America

Balboa Press rev. date: 7/20/2012

"In her book, *The Chatter That Matters*, Margaret takes us on an important journey – between our ears, out of our mouths, and deep within our hearts. By realizing we have "chatter" in our thoughts, our words, our actions and our values, we can positively control an outcome. She shows us that intentional awareness connected to intentional response can truly make a positive difference for ourselves, our families and our world."

Jolene Brown, CSP
Professional Speaker, Family Business Consultant and Author of "Sometimes You Need More Than a 2x4! How-to-tips to successfully grow a family business."

"The Chatter that Matters" is a how-to book for reclaiming control of your life. Margaret Martin offers both rules and tools for keeping your thoughts focused on only the things in your life that matter most, for the express purpose of creating more of them."

Lauren McLaughlin, author of "Go to ELF"
www.unitynow.com

I love thought-provoking activities that bring about beneficial transformation. Mind Chatter provides just that. It´s filled with an abundance of thought-enhancing activities all specifically designed to bring its readers to a much higher level of awareness and a much deeper level of choice. The author brings deliberate Light upon thoughts that deplete life and shows how to neutralize them effectively. The depth of planning and experience the author provides for the reader is comprehensive yet concise. The additional actions and directions offered to readers are also inspiring! The author's personal stories helped me relate firmly to my own challenges so much so that I believe other readers may find them equally as helpful. There are many suggested applications toward family, friends and business situations that add new dimension to activities one can engage in to expand one's transforming influences. All together, Mind Chatter does indeed take the reader toward very beneficial transformation. It's a great guidebook that you will want to reread regularly to help maintain the perfecting edge.

Dr. John S. Nagy, D. Min
Professional Coach, and Author of: Provoking Success,
Emotional Awareness Made
Easy and 5 other transformational books.

Preface

Your words are very powerful indeed. Are you aware of how powerful your words are? Seriously! Truly it is **Chatter Matters** in all that you do, from your **Mind Chatter** to the **Other Chatter** and the **Protection Chatter**, what you say in your mind – that self-talk, what you say to others and how you protect yourself from the negativity of others will define your life.

Think about how you use your words with others and how they use their words with you. Take just a few moments and reflect on what you have said and how you have said it within the last few hours.

This little exercise can open your eyes and perhaps your mind to the impact of what you say can and will have on those around you, from your family members to your co-workers and all points in between.

Now, take a moment and think about what others have said to you within the last few hours or even the previous 24 hours. What came up first? Was it positive or was it negative?

This little book has several purposes:

1) Help you take control of your **Mind Chatter** (Self-Talk), to turn the negative thoughts to empowering thoughts, the ability to change the negative words into empowering words.

2) To increase your awareness of your **Other Chatter** - communication with others, to help you realize the impact of how and what you say can have on the lives of people around you.

3) It is also a guide to help you with **Protection Chatter,** learn how to protect yourself from the impact of hurtful, negative words of others.

4) It will assist you in understanding how you use your words in being responsible and define your integrity – *Chatter Matters*.

Wouldn't you agree that when you experience positive words, hear a compliment or someone tells you that they really appreciate you, it does feel so good? It does make your heart soar doesn't it? It certainly causes my heart to soar and I feel so good. There is such wonderful energy created when we hear "good" words from others as well as from ourselves. It changes the energy flow in our bodies and brains to vibrate on a higher level.

I thank you for taking the time to go on *The Chatter that Matters* adventure and my hope is that it will give you the courage to use this information to help you become the person you want to be and to know that your words will create positive changes in your life.

Margaret Martin,
Clearwater, FL

Part One

Mind Chatter

aka - SELF TALK

You are what you think about whether you like it or not.

What do you hear in your mind all day? What do you hear when you think about your job, your health, your family? Do beat yourself up for having made a mistake, for being late, being overweight? Do you say or think things like:

I am so stupid

I am such a klutz

I hate my job

My job drives me crazy

My boss is a tyrant

I am fat

I don't have time to . . .

I can't afford . . . .

There are many other phrases I could add to this list, but you certainly do not need more phrases that you have not thought of yet.

Do you talk or think about your illness or disease? Or do you focus on health? Do you use someone else's labels to define who you are - ADD, OCD, and so on?

Here's something to consider: what you say and what you think about *is* what you bring into your life. As you think about the quote at the beginning of this section: "You are what you think about

1

whether you like it or not," understand that it is really true. It is the law of attraction. The Law of Attraction is defined by Esther and Jerry Hicks in their book by the same title, as: "That which is like unto itself; is drawn." And from the book *As a Man Thinketh* by James Allen, "As a man thinketh in his heart so is he."

"You will experience whatever you think after the words I AM . . ."

So what this really means is that which you think and talk about is drawn to you, even the things you don't want. The things you don't want, but talk about and think about, you give energy to, therefore bringing more of it to you. Such as "I just don't have time to . . .," "I want to get out of debt," "I can't afford it," "How am I going to pay for this, I have no money," and so on. The focus is on debt and lack of money, so that is where you put your energy and what you attract - debt and lack of money.

Take a moment and reflect on how else you would make your statement about money. Think about what and how you want things (money, health, and more) in your life, not about what your situation is at this moment, but what you want it to look like, what it will be. I encourage you to write down exactly what you want in each area of your life. Use the Life Design process as referred to in *Go to ELF* (ELF = Eternal Life Force) by Lauren McLaughlin. The Life Design process, write down: 1. What you want, 2. Why you want it, 3. How you will feel when you have it, and 4. What makes you believe you can have it for each item and 5. Let go of "how" it will happen, just trust that it will. have it for each item. Use the space below or at the back of the book in the notes section to begin your list:

Health _____

_____

_____

_____

_____

_____

_____

_____

_____

_____

_____

_____

_____

Financial _____

_____

_____

_____

_____

_____

_____

_____

_____

_____

_____

_____

_____

Margaret Martin

Career / Work _____

_____

_____

_____

_____

_____

_____

_____

_____

_____

_____

_____

Family / Relationships _____

_____

_____

_____

_____

_____

_____

_____

_____

_____

_____

_____

Personal Development _____

_____

_____

_____

_____

_____

_____

_____

_____

_____

_____

_____

Other _____

_____

_____

_____

_____

_____

_____

_____

_____

_____

_____

_____

Make a habit of thinking and talking about prosperity, about having money coming into your life, about having good health and well-being. For instance, a mantra you might use about money is *I always have as much as I need* or *I give myself permission to prosper.*

Form a habit of talking about your good health and focus on and create a mantra or "I am" statement such as *I have a vibrantly healthy body that is strong, flexible and toned* or *I am enjoying a healthy body that is fit, toned and flexible.*

In my experience I have noticed that most things people say to themselves are primarily negative. It is called the *Mind Chatter that Splatters.* People seem to constantly question themselves in their abilities, often putting themselves down, which is also shaming themselves. When you pause and honestly look at or evaluate the circumstance, you realize that yes, you really are capable and you do have the ability, intelligence, and knowledge to do and learn to do most anything you want to do. So why do you hold yourself back? Well, we have this *thing* in our mind that is often called the ego, monkey brain, or the inner critic. What is it with that inner critic, or *Mind Chatter* (ego) that we all have? Why are some people more affected by it than others?

For many, the inner critic is a constant experience and sometimes it is something they never overcome. It does take effort and the awareness to stop it when you hear it. "That Voice" shows up as you start a new project or want to create something new and "That Voice" says - *who do you think you are? Who's going to buy your product, your art? Who is going to believe you anyway?* and on and on . . . then you find yourself listening to "That Voice" and not completing your project. You give up believing in you, your true self, and instead believe what "That Voice" has said. You do this over and over and over again in every aspect of your life. From business to health, from relationships to self-care, from money to taking care of your home, the inner critic (ego), "The Voice" shows up.

The inner critic is often fueled by someone in your life who is or was your "outer critic." It could be a spouse, a teacher, a parent, a so-called friend who has been or is always there to criticize you, create more doubt, or remind you that *You aren't smart enough to do that, You are ugly, You will never amount to anything, You never get it right, Nobody in our family has ever . . . , You aren't good enough*, and so forth. Many times they are not necessarily saying these things with an intention to undermine you. They may have grown up this way and it has become a habit or in some cases the more successful they have become, the less assured they are, thus reducing their self-esteem.

Occasionally it is not that they are saying critical words, they may be correcting you constantly, wanting you to always do something their way, telling you that you could have cooked it better, you shouldn't do it that way or they would have done "it" differently. As you begin to have confidence in yourself, here comes the outer and inner critic, **negative *Mind Chatter***, to poke at you and it keeps telling you that you will never be a success anyway (or whatever), so why in the world should you try? That moves you back into self-doubt which often leads to you being immobilized. The situation creates a vicious circle. It keeps you down and bummed out. It really doesn't take much of that kind of thinking and you become paralyzed. You don't achieve those things that you say you really want to accomplish.

For example: When I was in junior high school (that is what we called middle school) after I took my first algebra test, I didn't do too badly, probably a B. After class the teacher said to me, "Margaret, you did not do as well as I thought you would, after all, your sister always did very well in my class." Well, that totally deflated me because I had studied and thought I was prepared for the test. And instead of using this incident as a challenge to outdo my sister, I did well enough to be in most classes with my friends. I never pushed harder, because I thought it would be a waste of my time, since the teachers compared me to her. So I allowed that incident to set the tone for my high school career and much of my life – nothing outstanding and always thinking that my sister was smarter than me. Is she smarter than me? I have no clue, but I do know that we approach most things differently which does not make one of us smarter than the other. Another result of that experience caused me to compare myself to others for most of my career. I would always look at other trainers or coaches and think that they did things better than me. One day after much healing, I had an "ah ha" moment, I realized they do things differently than me, not better. And in many cases, they learn from me.

Can you ever get out and overcome the inner critic? YES! How? It takes desire and action.

The desire to want to change and then the commitment to take action to change, takes believing yourself constantly to get things done. It takes courage to have the willingness to contradict the inner critic and to develop a plan to take action. Use these as action steps: desire, commitment and action. It can be as simple as repeating a mantra several times a day, such as: "I am a gift from the universe, compassionate, happy and committed to be . . . the best _____."

Please note: the point is to inspire you to take action; it is NOT about making you wrong. You are right where you are supposed to be, doing the best you can. And when you are repeating the mantra, allow yourself to experience the feeling the statement brings to you as if it was already a part of your life. It is very important to get into the feeling part, that sets your vibrational energy in motion – basically sending out vibes of what you want.

Many resources are available to help you get control of the inner critic, such as hiring a coach, working with a healer, taking courses on self-esteem, law of attraction, and success principles; learning to "let go;" reading books and being part of a mastermind group (more information in the resource section). Sometimes it may take various processes that are different for each person. Those can certainly be life-changing and help you finally believe in yourself.

There are some simple processes to master the inner critic that you can do on your own, but it is important to remember that you must be persistent and consistent in using it several times a day. One process that works is to sit quietly, focus on the area around your heart, breathe in deeply, slowly and focus your thoughts on your heart as if you are breathing through your heart, then remember a time of appreciation or love and focus on the feeling. Keep your focus on the feeling as you continue to breathe through your heart. And say one or a series of your affirmations. This only takes a few minutes. Do that several times a day. Very importantly, when you hear the inner critic at work that is a perfect time to pause and do the breathing exercise – it can take only seconds to do. Your focus will be renewed, as will your energy.

Another process is to catch yourself thinking or talking negatively and change the words immediately. Change things such as "my body is fighting an infection" to "my body is healing; I have a healthy _____ (whatever is ill)." Move from "I am always late" to "I am arriving on time." "I really struggle with my weight" to "I maintain healthy weight for my body." Everything you say negatively, you can change it to positive, empowering words.

> *"A person is literally what they think, their character*
> *being the complete sum of all of their thoughts."*
> . . . James Allen

Below, or on a separate paper, make two columns. Title one Negative and one Empowering. Then list all the negative things that you know that you say to yourself or others in the Negative column. When you have finished that list, go back to each statement and change it to an empowering statement or word.

Negative_____

_____

_____

_____

_____

_____

_____

_____

_____

_____

_____

_____

_____

Empowering_____

_____

_____

_____

_____

_____

_____

_____

_____

_____

_____

_____

_____

You can create affirmations for yourself from this list to read or repeat aloud every day, two to three times a day or you may choose from one of my audio affirmations I have recorded which you will find on my website.

Reading affirmations every day, especially early in the morning to start your day is the best time. It will get you motivated, excited and give your brain the information that will help you change the thought pattern. As you say your affirmations, you will want to add in the feeling of excitement / get all jazzed up / create a buzz about this affirmation. What about it gets you excited? Add that feeling to this process – it only takes a few extra seconds and will further help cement it into your thought process. You can also visualize what it looks like when you are thinking the way that you want to add to your life.

Several pages ago you wrote down the What, Why, How I will feel, and Why I believe for various things you want in your life – this is very similar. As you say your affirmation, think about how you feel when you have it.

Do the exercise of reading these affirming statements every morning for 30 days and you will definitely see a positive change. It is well proven that to succeed in developing a new habit, you must do it for minimum of 30 days. Also, I suggest reading or listening to your affirmations right before you sleep – your sub-conscious mind will work on them for you.

The work of Louise Hay, *You Can Heal Your Life*, is outstanding, and the workbook *Love Yourself, Heal Your Life* is excellent to process more in-depth to heal your life. A very important process that came from her work is the Mirror Exercise - talk positively to yourself first thing in the morning, throughout the day and then again at night before you go to bed. Tell yourself what you are proud of accomplishing for that day (even if it's only that you smiled at a stranger); then tell yourself "I love you."

Most people feel that this is one of the hardest processes to do. There are so many people who really never look at themselves and appreciate their body, their abilities and their talents. Think about it. Your body does a lot for you each day, keeping you alive with your heart pumping consistently without ever asking whether you want it to or not. Even when you have added other things that make it work harder, such as extra weight, smoking, not enough or any exercise and much more your body keeps on working. If nothing else, you can thank your body for getting you through the day. Thank all of the trillions of cells that keep you functioning and thriving. Then you can gradually add looking into your eyes and seeing that there is a truly magnificent person reflecting back at you – one that does some pretty amazing things that rarely ever gets appreciated by its owner.

Do this exercise for 30 days and you will be amazed at what a positive change it will make in your life; more confidence and more enthusiasm.

This experience has increased my awareness as to how many people still struggle with the inner critic wearing them down and beating them up and it continues to inspire me to help as many people as possible to learn these processes of how to control and get rid of the inner critic. It further inspires my mission: To help individuals in making a positive difference, positive changes in their own lives.

There are some very simple processes that when used consistently will rid you of most of the negative self-talk. You can do this yourself. It takes dedication, persistence and a willingness to change.

Without true belief in yourself, it will be more difficult to accomplish those things that you really want.

> *"Until you make peace with who you are, you'll*
> *never be content with what you have."*
> *. . . Doris Mortman*

"There is neither good nor bad, but thinking
makes it so."
. . . *Shakespeare*

"I'm a devout believer that paying attention to our
self-talk is vitally important for our mental health."
. . . *Jill Bolte Taylor*

I know this healing process works when you really put the effort into it because it has worked for me. It has taken me years of healing work after I was out of the surroundings of consistent criticism and I do continue my healing process each day. I worked with an intuitive healer – Peggy Rometo, read lots of books and took various courses, and one of the pivotal times in my life came when I attended a workshop facilitated by Jack Canfield in the summer of 2007, *Breakthrough to Success*, and while there really put myself into the various processes that we did and I came home a changed person. (This is an outstanding program and I attended for my own personal development as well as a train-the-trainer program to add to the resources in my work.) Some people didn't notice because for years I covered my lack of belief in me - I sounded very confident, but inside was always second-guessing myself. Many did notice because I had a different energy within and surrounding me. So when I shared with my friends that I had finally gotten rid of that inner critic that had been hanging around for many, many years, they replied, "Well Margaret, I've believed in you for years." And I replied to them, "Yes, I know and I am very grateful, but what is really important is that I now believe in me."

Give belief in yourself a try, do it consistently for 30 days and you will see the difference too! Set up a schedule, a daily ritual or habit to set these processes into place and the most important piece is having the courage to follow it diligently and consistently for 30 days, without a waiver to the schedule.

It will be helpful to have a support system, an accountability partner or a friend with whom you are in contact daily, to keep them posted on your progress as well as they can boost you up when you get discouraged. I not only had an accountability partner to help me, I asked my best friend too. Having that support makes all the difference in helping you accomplish your goals.

How you start and end your day makes a huge difference in your life. Here is an idea of a possible schedule:

6:00am - Awaken

6:10 am – Sitting quietly in "your space" begin the day by being grateful for the start of a new day and your blessings – you can write this down in your journal or say it mentally or aloud. Then spend about 10 – 15 minutes reading. Read something uplifting. There are many choices – some people read from A Course in Miracles, the Bible or other spiritual book of their faith. (Other options and suggestions can be found on the Reading List section of my website.) The point is to start your day in an uplifting manner.

6:20 am – Meditate, Pray or just sit quietly for a minimum of 5 minutes, preferably 15 – 30 minutes or longer if it fits for you. Then spend at least 2-3 minutes visualizing how you will spend your day and what your ultimate goal or work is and what you will be doing. Don't worry about the how (how you will accomplish it or get it done) here, just focus on the vision. Repeat or listen to your affirmations for the day.

6:35 am – Do some exercise, if not then, commit to something later in the day

This is just a suggestion and is adjustable by what time you need to get to work or get children to school, but the key point is that you could spend as little as 15 – 20 extra minutes in the morning to get your day started on the right track.

I shared this recently in a workshop on Stress Management and a few weeks later I was back at the company providing a workshop on Conflict Resolution and shared again how important it is to start and end your day well, even if it is only taking an extra 5 minutes for yourself in the morning. When one participant said that he didn't have time to do that, another popped up and said, "I have started taking just 5 minutes for me in the morning with a cup of coffee. It makes a positive difference in my day." Yay! I was so excited that she was able to tell him that it was easier than he thought!

Equally important is to take a few minutes to end your day well – many people watch the evening news right before bedtime and wonder why they cannot sleep. (Note, the news is often filled with negativity which causes the viewer stress and anxiety. If you are like that, you probably would want to change your routine or add some quiet positive reading after the broadcast is over.) Here is a suggestion to do about 10 to 30 minutes before you turn out the lights. Get a special journal, what I call a Gratitude Journal (something I have done for many years) to keep on your bedside table; write the date and then list 3 – 5 things for which you are grateful that happened that particular day – could be something like – a phone conversation with your best friend, a rose bush you saw has the most magnificent flowers today, you had mostly green lights in today's driving, saw a beautiful sunset, enjoyed a job well done today. During the writing of gratitudes, reflect on your day, how did it go, what was a success, what needed improvement? Make a note of the achievements in your journal.

Ending your day on a positive frame of mind is definitely important and it is a little easier when you have written down those things for which you are grateful.

> *"I give myself permission to sleep well*
> *and awaken well rested."*
> *. . . Margaret Martin*

"If a fellow isn't thankful for what he's got, he isn't likely to be thankful for what he's going to get."
. . . Frank A. Clark

"God gave you a gift of 86,400 seconds today. Have you used one to say 'thank you'?"
. . . William Arthur Ward

Part Two

Other Chatter

USING YOUR WORDS WITH OTHERS

For a moment focus on how you recently used your words with others; with your families, friends, co-workers and those just regular people in your lives (cashiers, janitors, and so on). Much of how you talk to people evolves from how you were raised or learned in school, some of it really good, some of it not. As you read this, I encourage you to think about the verbal interaction that you have had with people so far today - - - - - - - - - - - - - - - and next reflect on yesterday's interactions; - - - - - - - - - - then ask yourself this question, "Was my communication to others overall a positive experience for all involved?" "Did I say what needed to be said to the best of my ability?" If not, what could you have done differently to make it a better situation?

You may want to jot those down:_____

_____

_____

_____

_____

_____

_____

_____

_____

_____

Let's begin to look at the impact of your words on others. First, are you genuine when you talk with others? It really is about being real, saying only what you mean, speaking with truth to others in a manner of care and love. You can say what you really mean in truth even when it is a negative situation, by paying attention to how you say it. You always have a choice at every given moment as to how you will interact with people and when you have the responsibility as a parent, coach, mentor, teacher, supervisor, or company owner, how you say what needs to be said will have a major impact on the recipient.

Everyone reading this book has experienced the wonderful feeling of appreciation when someone says something nice to you or about you. I hope you have also had the experience of when you've done something wrong and the person in charge handled the situation with care to help you see what or how things could have turned out differently. By experiencing a situation such as that, you are encouraged to continue doing the best you know how to do.

You also know that when you are that person in charge, how much better you feel when you have had to handle a negative situation with someone and you did it with care. You know that when you react in frustration and anger, it really only makes the matter worse.

Several years ago, I was in charge of a project for my homeowner's association – we were doing some major renovations which included re-roofing all of our buildings. We were several days into that part of the project when I questioned our roofing consultant about the men doing the job – for whom did they work? I soon discovered that they were sub-contractors which was a violation in the contract with the roof contractor. I was really upset because our contract stated that if the contractor was going to use sub-contractors, we were to be notified and could choose not to use their subs. In discussions such as this, I always had another member of the Board of Directors with me so that all communication was clear. So I asked this consultant if he had always known that we had subs on the job. His response was, "yes," I then said to him, "Are you aware that this is not only a violation of our contract with the roof contractor, it is a violation of your contract with us and you could be fired?" (Note: even though I was quite upset, I kept my tone and volume of voice on an even keel.) He said that he was aware of the situation. I then told him that we (the other Board member and I) would have to discuss it with the other Board members, but until then I would recommend that he stay on the job because up to that point, he had provided effective work. I reminded him that he must be absolutely clear in his conversation and make sure no further violations happened. (After discussing it with the other members of the Board, we did keep the roofing consultant on the job and he caught a few things that could have cost a great deal more money and time during the project.)

This is an example of how you can handle situations that are difficult where tempers could usually flair creating a very difficult situation for everyone. The main key here is to keep a level head, step back take a deep breath and proceed with care.

Another, yet very different example, I read recently in the materials of a training program that I was facilitating on Conflict Resolution in which the group was discussing how our expectations of others are generally self-fulfilling prophecies. This story is an excellent example of this type of verbal interaction.

> A college professor experimented with three of her college classes to see if she could cause self-fulfilling prophecy. When she graded the first exam, the average grade was the same for three of her business and professional communication courses. When she returned the papers to the first class, she praised them for their high grades and intelligent, thoughtful answers. While returning papers to the second class, the professor neither praised nor criticized the class. However, while returning papers to the third

class, she severely reprimanded the students for having the lowest grades she had ever seen and for giving thoughtless, undeveloped answers. No further mention of the exam grades was mentioned and the classes continued as usual.

The results of the second exam were surprising: the grades from the class that had been praised were much better than on the first exam; the class that was neither praised nor criticized was about the same; and the grades of the class that had been severely criticized were much worse than on the first exam.

Feeling bad about what had happened; the professor told the class what she had done. Nobody believed her! The improved class said they made better grades because they were better students. The class with the poor grades said she was just trying to make them feel better; they knew they were truly poor students.

This experiment by the professor will probably have a lasting effect on the first and the third groups of students. The first group will continue feeling / thinking that they are smart and do things well. Yet, the third group may have a lasting negative affect as they continue through school and into the workplace with probably a lower self-esteem all because a professor decided to experiment with them without their being aware of the process. How could she have done a better job of the situation?

Since this is not my area of expertise, I am providing you with the ideas that came to me as I was discussing this with the group. My suggestion is the first step she should have taken would have been to notify the department head that she was going to do the experiment so that at least there would be a record of what she was doing which would help the third group of students understand that it was an experiment. Another idea would include having another professor do the same experiment, but in reverse; saying to the third group that they were the excellent students, having praised their grades.

The point here is to be aware of what you say to others and the potential impact it can have on the recipient of your communication.

Children

The above story of the professor is certainly appropriate here as we talk about a parent's inter-action with their child/children.

If you are a parent, you have a huge responsibility. To speak to your children with love and care sometimes is very, very hard and there is probably not one of us, who as a parent, has not lost our patience, our temper and spewed words of anger and frustration to our children. When this happens, it is how you respond to them after that situation that makes such a difference.

One of the things I learned to do is to apologize to your children when you lose control. It does not right the wrong, but it helps them to better understand that when their parent has overreacted. And that you have taken a few moments to reflect and realize that you did not do the right thing. If you have the courage to apologize, and it takes courage, and let them know that you wish you had not said or done what you did, you will begin to think before you speak and develop new habits. To be clear here, this is not an action that excuses what the child has done or said that resulted in your overreaction, it is about your overreaction. From what I have learned, many children have negative behavior to get the attention of their parents. We all want attention, to be loved, and sometimes any attention is better than no attention even if it is negative.

Remember that your expectations and communication with your children and all children with whom you come in contact can give them the confidence to do well in all that they do or not. It really is a simple process, yet so hard for so many.

If you are someone who loses their patience often, take your child and hug them, it helps both of you heal. And besides, I don't think we get enough hugs every day.

Much more could be discussed here, but I am certainly not the parenting expert, only a mother who did the best she could under whatever circumstances were there at the time. Suffice it to say that clearly the message is to make your *Chatter Matter* especially with your children. Remember there are many resources available to help you be a better parent – seek them out.

And to the teachers out there, I would ask that you carefully refrain from judging or having negative expectations of your students. I am sure that it is tough to do and teaching children is certainly not my area of expertise – I teach adults in various workshops and training program. I have to do the same thing with adults, look at all of them as objectively as I can. I work diligently at being conscious of the words I communicate so as to be clear, yet build up the participants and help them see themselves more clearly.

Employees

When you are the boss, no matter what your title is, and you have to deal with employees who have created a negative situation and I think the best way to handle this is not to yell at them or say anything that dehumanizes them. Saying demoralizing things and yelling only makes for a huge negative situation for all, and there are many people that find this to be very hard to do.

As the employer / manager, you realize that certainly the employee did not do this on purpose The best thing to do is to take a step back and look at the situation with an attitude of "how can I make this better," not to demean the person by saying things like, "You are so stupid, always messing up," or "I can't believe you would do this again, what's the matter with you anyway?" or something similar. Unless you have the intention to create a bad state of affairs for all involved. Always take them aside, tell them in private the impact of what they did, what a mess it created. (Criticize in Private; Praise in Public.) Then ask them, "What can I do to help you prevent this from happening again?" By offering to help, you show you care about them and want them to do and be their best. Which makes it a win-win for all.

The difficult part of leadership sometimes is realizing you do not have all the "right" answers immediately and once in a while, you say the wrong thing. It may be best to ask for forgiveness, let it go and move on to improve the next situation that shows up.

If you are in the habit of yelling / raising your voice / saying things like "If you don't like the rules around here, that's too bad, don't let the door hit you on the way out," or have an attitude that you are doing folks a favor to hire them – then I suggest a major attitude shift for you. We humans are all pretty much the same – we want love / respect / kindness in our lives and REALLY, how hard can it be to show the people that work for you some kindness and respect? After all, if it were not for them, you would not have a business!

Here is a different perspective – think about this, when you overreact at someone / yell at them / say dehumanizing things – it is about you. It is about what is going on in your life, not the person at whom you are yelling. Their action may have triggered something in you causing your negative response. So get a grip on yourself! Take a good look at what it was that triggered you into overreaction. That will be an excellent discovery for you. Then upon that discovery, the next time someone does or says something to "push your button;" you can take a deep breath, or three, and respond, not react.

By following some of these suggestions, you can experience an improved relationship with your employees or those that you manage.

Social

Social situations are most interesting when it comes to conversations and the communication with others. When you really pay attention to conversations that you have with others, especially in social situations, do you feel that you have really had a "real" conversation? In most cases I find that the majority of people are not real / authentic in their "party talk." And that is generally what social situations are about, which is totally okay. Sometimes people just say things that they think we want to hear and others seem concerned only with what others will think about them and what they say, they worry about whether they are wearing the right outfit (that's most women).

Don't you generally say "I am fine or I am great" when someone asks you how you are, even when you may have a headache, be tired, or feeling out of sorts? Is that wrong? Not necessarily, because it is probably not appropriate to go on and on about your problems with others – would you want someone else doing that to you? If it is a good friend, you might say, "I'm doing well, dealing with a bit of a headache, but glad I'm here to forget about it." When you say something in that manner to a friend, they will usually feel compassionate and glad that you are focused on a positive outcome. Plus, a statement like that puts you into a positive focus of releasing the headache instead of focusing on the pain.

Often we get hung up that we will be judged by others. The reality is that we all judge each other, that is human nature. For instance, when you catch yourself judging others, take a step back, make it an observation instead of a judgment - notice it and move on. When we judge others, we present ourselves as better than the one we are judging. Gossip happens when you engage others in your judgment. Another perspective is just that, your thoughts and judgments are your perspective which can be, and usually is, different from others. The best action, show up and be who you really are, take the judgments of others lightly, and release any critical / judgmental thoughts toward others. After all, do we have the right to judge others? No, not really; perhaps remembering not to judge someone until you have walked a mile in their shoes (if they are blessed to have shoes.) The only way you can walk in someone else's shoes is to take yours off first.

*"We are all inclined to judge ourselves by our ideals,
others by their acts."......
... Harold Nicolson*

I do think it is absolutely delightful when you can get into a great engaging conversation at a party. It creates such wonderful interaction, gets people thinking and can build new friendships or business opportunities. Plus it can be just fun to have random conversations. I find that many times I learn more than I ever thought I would.

In General

A very important thing to note: pay attention to how you converse with people when you are tired and / or frustrated, especially your family members. Often people take for granted that they can just say anything they want to their family with total disregard as to the impact of their words.

A while ago I happened to watch a talk show that was focusing on how a group of men talked to their wives. Even though I know this happens and have been a recipient as well, I was amazed at how cruel these men were (and men are not alone in inflicting verbal abuse). When questioned about why he degraded and humiliated his wife, one man replied, "Because I can." This is so amazing and unfortunately true. When this happens, it usually is a person who has a low self regard, a person who has also been degraded or abused, and to feel better about himself or herself, he or she has to bring the other person down as far as possible. Sometimes people feel threatened and the only way for them to get a handle on things is to put others down, call them names, to ridicule them or take other types of negative actions.

We see more and more bullying behavior in children and teenagers. There seems to be a lot more of that going on these days with very few people stepping in to help. (Well, I am not sure if there is more bullying going on, perhaps finally there is an increased awareness.) I think there are many reasons why people don't step in to help is the common phrase, "I just don't want to get involved." But what if it was your child who was getting beat up or being made fun of, would that make a difference? The fear of retribution is also a huge concern too for people not wanting to get involved. This encourages the perpetrator to keep on and perhaps become the husband or wife who is the abuser. There have been so many news accounts of people, even many children, taking their lives because they did not see another way out, another way to get relief.

We had a situation in our own family that I found difficult to figure out best how to handle – when my daughter was in middle school two of the girls in her class were always saying cruel things to her and most days she would burst into tears on the way home. Instead of going to the parents, who I didn't think would believe that their daughters would do this, or confront the girls about their actions, which could have created more harm than good, I talked with her. We talked about why we thought these girls were being cruel, about what they were saying and whether there was any truth in words, and we talked about of her positive attributes as well as how courageous she was not to stoop to their level. This was a very difficult time for both of us – she wanted to lash out at them, I wanted to yell at these girls and their parents. Which was the right way to handle it, I am still not sure. I am glad that at least at this point in time the girls have grown up and don't act like that and are on good speaking terms with my daughter.

One of the best things that I have found to do is to tell those you love and care about, that you do care and love them each day. Tell people that you appreciate them. As we all know, life is short – sometimes shorter than we plan and I know that I would not want something to happen to a family member or friend knowing that I never told them how much they mean to me. Make at least one day a week that you will designate as a "random act of appreciation day" and tell each person with whom you interact that you appreciate them for the work that they do. You may feel foolish at first, but once you have done this for a while, it will become second nature to you and you will enjoy seeing the positive impact it has on people. Telling people such as the cleaning woman in your office building, the person bagging your groceries, the lawn maintenance crew and so on. Make a game out of it. You will be surprised how delighted you help people to feel. - - - Just one more way to make the world a better place. Who knows what the actual impact could be, you may be saving someone's life!

Other People's Judgment

As a society in general, we tend to be very critical and quick to judge others. I touched a bit on this in the previous section, but let's take a deeper look into how much negativity there is in our judgments.

Look at the media coverage and then listen to the conversations of others making all types of judgments about people and their actions. Movie stars, hit singers, other public figures get a lot of media coverage. Do you really care about what they are doing? It is really important to your life? What impact does it have on you and the rest of us when one of them has become out of control from drugs or alcohol? Somehow they have been put on a pedestal and we tend to think that they should make no mistakes. Frankly, it is none of your business. More than likely, in their rise to stardom they were not prepared for the intense scrutiny of their lives. Could you handle it? I am not sure that I would like it. How would you handle it if every time you walked out your door, got in your car, went out to eat there was a sea of photographers and on-lookers with cell cams just waiting to take a picture of your every move because if you slip up and they have it first, they will make money, they will be newsworthy. My personal opinion: what a sad state of affairs we are in when that has become our focus.

The concern about being judged by others does create a problem for most people - you allow the possibility of what other people "might" think about you to keep you from living your life in a way that is in your best interest or to do the things that you think are best for you, you hold yourself back out of the fear that others maybe quick to judge you, your efforts or your work – I know that one well. Even some of the simple things that you do can cause you to worry about what others think. This often begins in school, (remember the story of the professor's experiment on self-fulfilling prophecies) usually starts in elementary school and then the cruelest time of judging or making fun of someone else gets worse in middle school and high school. You may have been the recipient of that type of judging and what often results in bullying. Hardly any of us escaped from some sort of intense judgment of others and for some, it totally changed your life – not necessarily in a good way.

In all that I have learned through the years, the intense judging and bullying is the result of an individual or group of people not feeling good about themselves. They may be filled with fear of being vulnerable and when we are feeling vulnerable, we are not in control. Putting others down is one way to "feel in control" and mistakenly thought to make the taunter feel better. It does not cause them to feel better in the long run. More often, the bully has been bullied either at home or by someone else somewhere along the way. The bottom line: it is how you feel on the inside that will determine how you treat others.

You may also have been one of those who did the taunting / bullying. If you were the taunter, I hope that you have received help, gotten over it and no longer judge and criticize to hurt others in order for you to feel accepted, liked and worthy. I will encourage you to become an advocate to help others, especially young men and women, to have the courage to make the necessary changes that will lead to happiness. If not, please get some help; there are many resources readily available these days.

Our desire for peace must be stronger than our
attachment to our misery, our
ego or our need to be right.

"When you let go of your doubts, insecurities, prejudices,
and judgments – even if it is just for a moment – you
transcend your ego's limits and reconnect with who you
really are and why you are here."

. . . Peggy Rometo,
the Little Book of Big Promises

Gossip

Do you gossip? Most of us do whether we admit it or not. Yes, I forget sometimes and get caught up in the stories about others, then fortunately I catch myself. When I do catch myself, I may try to change the topic, sometimes just stop participating in the conversation, or even walk away and find a more enlightening conversation.

In observing a group of people - friends or neighbors - conversations often evolve to the "stories" about others and most often the people that are missing from the group. Sometimes it starts out as an update about everyone who is there. Then if something is "happening" in someone's life, often it becomes a focus of conversation.

If the conversation about a specific person is shared as information then it can be perceived as information update. If not and you get into "did you know . . .;" "have you heard . . . .;" "can you believe . . . ????" Or perhaps it shifts to judging or comparing. In addition to a "can you believe this" type of conversation takes on a life of its own and then it is gossip. The question is "What good has it done and/or what has it accomplished?" Nothing positive. And really, would you say these things about them if they were present? Of course not! Would you want them getting into a conversation like that about you? I don't think so . . . probably not.

Generally, people really do not mean to be vicious or create any harm to others. Gossiping often is a habit because they can't think of other things to talk about.

You probably remember the telephone game from childhood? The first person in a line whispered something in the next person's ear, they then whispered in the next person's ear, and so on. Rarely did the ending statement resemble the beginning statement. This type of exaggeration still happens today when you don't rein it in and let it continue; especially when you contribute to it. Be careful what you say about others because it can easily be taken out of context by those in hearing range. If you put yourself in the other person's shoes, would you want a conversation like that being continuously spread around about you? When you stop and think about it, it definitely gives you a better perspective about your participation in gossip.

Next time the opportunity comes around, I suggest that you give it more thought and opt out and say to the others involved perhaps what is being said might have been exaggerated since you were not there and don't know the real facts. It does take courage to do this and people may look at you strangely at first. You are raising your standards and values to not be a contributor to the harm of someone else. You may even be a good example for others – wouldn't that feel good? A word of caution here, when you say that you are not participating in the story, aka gossip, do not say it in a haughty, "I'm better than you" manner because that will certainly defeat the purpose.

What are some other topics you might talk about instead of talking about others (gossiping)?

List some here:_____

_____

_____

_____

_____

_____

_____

_____

_____

_____

_____

_____

_____

Part Three

Points to ponder . . .

Are you kind when talking to others?

I know that when I am in what I call *direct mode,* getting to the point quickly without always putting the words into a "soft" manner may be perceived as unkind. It is not that I am being unkind; I am just distributing information quickly. At least that is my intention. What often happens is that the recipient of that information feels as if they have been slammed; not my intention.

I did not realize for many years how it was impacting others. Now with this awareness, I am most always very conscious to pay attention to the impact my words have on others. Perhaps you fit this description, if so you will want to give more attention to the manner in which you talk with others. When you are kind in your words, even though they may have a powerful impact, the more likely that your words will be heard and received by others with the intention we desire.

Because I am direct and honest when talking with people, some are surprised at first. I don't beat around the bush, I say what is appropriate (from my perspective) and in a direct manner. Many a friend has said, "You always know where you stand with Margaret." Actually, I am pleased that people feel that way because there have been so many times that I feel something is amiss with someone, yet they don't tell me or at least advise me that things in their life are a little "out of kilter" right now, or that I have done or said something that hurt them.

Sometimes people may act friendly when their intention is not friendship. I do not like not knowing where I stand with people – I feel out of my comfort zone, as if I am on eggshells waiting for something else to happen. If someone has caused me to be upset, I do my best to talk with them and see what the situation is. It is certainly better to meet it head on than to wonder . . . that wastes a lot of time and energy.

For example, one of my business colleagues sent me an email the other day asking my opinion on how to handle a particular situation. The basics of the situation: the colleague had bid on a certain project; things looked good that she would be awarded the project and everything was moving along smoothly. All of a sudden communication came to an abrupt halt – no updates, no returned emails or phone calls. My colleague was frustrated, bewildered as to what had happened. The colleague then sent me an email and asked my help on what would be the best way to handle this. My response, we needed to talk about it and then scheduled the time. One thing that I reminded her during our conversation is that "we don't know what is happening on the other end." Life happens while we are doing our work in the world. After we discussed the situation, I suggested that she call and set up an appointment to talk with the individual in charge of the project and just ask what happened. If that individual refused, then drop it; there is probably nothing that you can do at this point. It will keep your reputation in tact. Well, she emailed me later that day to let me know she had talked with the project leader and found out the project had not only changed locations, but the project leader was overwhelmed with dealing with all of the quick, necessary changes and my colleague is still on for her part in completing the project.

You can waste a whole lot of time and energy just wondering what happened. This includes business and personal stuff. One of the best suggestions I can give is to just take a deep breath and step into the courage to gently meet the situation head on, and then you will usually have clarity about the other person's point of view or their situation. Otherwise, you will just stew about it for hours on end and get nothing accomplished. My colleague was able to get the situation resolved and fortunately in her favor, but if she had not won the contract, she would have been able to move on with an answer as to why not.

Are you mean-spirited when you talk with others?

Well, you might confuse being direct with being mean-spirited, but there is a significant difference. To clarify, being mean-spirited is someone who is bad-tempered, belligerent or malicious, according to Encarta Dictionary. This type of word use is very different from direct. Most often this happens when people are feeling less confident in themselves and are quick to verbally attack someone because of something they have perceived is an injustice toward them or someone else they care about. One thing to note here is that we easily misperceive other people's situation. Just because a woman is pretty, well-dressed, has glowing skin, and beautiful hair, doesn't mean she has everything going right in her life. Nor does it mean that the man with rumpled clothes, who is sloppily dressed, and could use a better haircut is not smart nor very good at his job or even possibly a former high profile executive who has hit hard times and is a good friend to those in his life.

We are quick to misjudge and when we are feeling down on ourselves it may seem like a good idea to make snide or bitter comments about others who do not present themselves as we "think" they should. Usually it is something that should not have been said at all. And the perpetrator does not feel any better after he or she has said mean-spirited statement. There are so many examples of this in movies, television and books. There are a number of people, whether young or older, who think they have a right to put others down; let's be clear, no one has that right. In the movies, books and television the "bad" guys usually learn their lesson, but that is not often the case in real life. Some people go their whole life putting others down, being rude, verbally attacking others and never take the time to learn how not to do that. I think they are afraid, afraid of what they may discover and just don't want to take a chance of experiencing more pain, so they stay in fear mode.

Recently there has been a lot of discussion about confronting the bully in schools. This is an important issue and I am glad to see schools and parents addressing it. The school bully becomes the workplace bully and even the bully in their household, and if you have ever worked with one of them, it is a miserable experience until someone has the courage to confront them. And for clarification, bullies come in all sizes, shapes and are men, women, and children. So, when you are upset or angry, give a lot of thought to the impact your words are having on the recipient(s), don't be a bully or mean-spirited. If you do fit this example, please get some help. You will be much happier in the long run.

Are the receivers of your words shrinking away, their eyes welling with tears, or perhaps getting angry with the way they are being treated? Have you experienced criticisms or someone else's anger? You then know what I am talking about. (The previous talk-show reference is an example.) Sometimes your communication style has become a habit and you may not even be aware of it. For example, many years ago when I was working in a corporate setting as an administrative assistant to the branch manager of a financial services company, I received a call from one of his clients. The man was an elderly man who rudely barked out orders to me, "You will get me the . . . and then you will do this and that." There was not a pleasant word coming out of his mouth and just so that you know, this was not during any kind of financial crisis; it is just the way he treated people every time he called. (Note, this is different than being direct with your words.) Well, I replied, "Mr. So-and-so, I'll be happy to get that information for you, but please do not talk to me in that manner." (Note – I said that in a very nice manner, not demanding.) I ended the conversation pleasantly, advising Mr. So-and-so that I would call him back shortly with the information. As you might imagine, my boss was standing in front of me with his eyes bugging out for having said that to his client (I did understand the possible implications, he could lose the man as a client). So I looked at him, and because I worked in an open area with others, I said, "Well, I guess we need to go to the kitchen and talk." I explained to him that I was not going to be verbally abused anymore, that the company did not pay me enough money to take that kind of abuse, even if they paid me millions I would not, and if he wanted to fire me then please do. I said to him that his client had probably developed the habit of talking to people like that and possibly wasn't even aware of it. He did not fire me, but he arranged for someone else in the office to take Mr. So-and-so's calls and I guess Mr. So-and-so is still rudely barking out orders to people in a dehumanizing way.

Give some thought to your communication style and assess how you are giving instructions or directions to see if you have developed bad habits in communicating. Ask others to provide you with their feed back. Keep in mind, you want them to be honest so that you can learn. You will then realize that you do not have to continue in that habit any longer. Make a decision not to treat people badly, take action to change this behavior, there are many options such as hiring a coach, getting therapy, reading books on self-help, getting an accountability partner (check the resources for an explanation of how this works) to work with you in the steps that you plan to take to make the necessary changes. It can be done; it just means making a commitment to change and sticking to it. Do so and you will feel much better about yourself and others will enjoy being around you more. I will add, all of us get angry or upset once in a while, that is being human, you have the ability as a human being to make the choice as to how you will *respond* and handle the situation with thought, care and grace.

List 3 ways or things that you recall having said badly.

1. _____
_____
_____
_____

2. _____
_____
_____
_____

3. _____
_____
_____
_____

Now, take those statements and rewrite them in a way that would communicate better.

1. _____
_____
_____
_____

2. _____
_____
_____
_____

3. _____
_____
_____
_____

More notes:_____

_____

_____

_____

_____

_____

_____

_____

_____

_____

_____

_____

Part Four

What's Your Love Chatter?

Love and Appreciation

*"Love is a fabric that never fades, no matter how often
it is washed n the water of adversity and grief."*
... Anonymous

*"You come to love not by finding the perfect person, but
by seeing an imperfect person perfectly."*
... Sam Keen

What words do you use to express love / appreciation / care / kindness? Don't you really enjoy hearing someone tell you how much they love you, appreciate you or care about you? More and more research is being done on how important it is to our world that we love others - or as we have heard for thousands of years - love your neighbor as yourself. Do you do that? Love can be expressed in many ways; to tell someone how much you appreciate them is just one way of expressing love. Love is not always about romance, as I am sure that you are aware, so the more often we can tell others that we love them in some manner the better our world will be. Just look at the research by Masaru Emoto has done on the impact of words on the molecular structure of water.

"What is the photograph of frozen water crystals? It was 1994 when the idea to freeze water and observe it with microscope came upon me. With this method, I was convinced that I should be able to see something like snow crystals.

After two months of trial and error, this idea bore fruit. The beautifully shining hexagonal crystals were created from the invisible world. My staff at the laboratory and I were absorbed in it and began to do many researches.

At first, we strenuously observed crystals of tap water, river water, and lake water. From the tap water we could not get any beautiful crystals. We could not get any beautiful ones from rivers and lakes near big cities, either. However, from the water from rivers and lakes where water is kept pristine from development, we could observe beautiful crystals with each one having its own uniqueness.

The observation was done in various ways:

- Observe the crystal of frozen water after showing letters to water
- Showing pictures to water
- Playing music to water
- Praying to water

In all of these experiments, distilled water for hospital usage produced by the same company was used. Since it is distilled twice, it can be said that it is pure water.

The result was that we always observed beautiful crystals after giving good words, playing good music, and showing, playing, or offering pure prayer to water. On the other hand, we observed disfigured crystals in the opposite situation. Moreover, we never observed identical crystals."

Check the resource page for links to his website and more information.

The words you say to others always have more of an impact than you ever expect that they will. Make sure that each day you tell at least one someone that you care or that you appreciate them. The words you use with children are so important and will have lasting impact on the little ones and I know that I was not always at my best when speaking with my children. I am much more aware now and try very hard to put care in action when talking.

If you would spend a few seconds expressing yourself from your heart, you would feel so much better and so would those who receive those words. Heartfelt words impact us more positively. Spend some time loving and appreciating "YOU" for all that you do and for being who you are.

In thinking about the phrase "love your neighbor as yourself," it is an important part of what we "should" be doing, we have heard it all our lives. I don't know about you, but I know or encounter people who are darned hard to love; you might have had a similar experience. Well, I have decided to let go of the *need* to love them and just do my best at being kind. I think if I can just be kind to them, I think that is a step in the right direction.

In discussing this with a few people, there have been some interesting perspectives. One man said that there are some people whose behavior / actions / comments are such that he doesn't feel that he can be kind to them, much less love them. I suggested that he think about whether he could embrace being kind without judgment – time will tell and it is certainly his choice. Perhaps he could spend a few moments in reflection as to why that is such a difficult concept to embrace. Many others like the idea of being kind to those who are hard to love – at least you are putting out some positive energy. On a daily basis almost every one of us has an opportunity to express / show kindness to others, including the experiences we encounter through work, volunteering, commuting to / from our various events and the people in our neighborhoods, so we need to make the decision to do it – just be kind as best you can.

Many people complain about how much there is wrong in their community and the world, yet they are not doing anything to make it better. Do they really have the "right" to do so? Well of course they have the right of free speech, yet the point to convey here is that if you want to have more love and kindness in the world, then you have to be a part of the change, part of the process to make it a better place. I love Gandhi's quote, "You must be the change you want to see in the world." So start somewhere today being kinder to others, perhaps even start doing random acts of kindness at least once a week. You will feel better and so will they.

What Encouraging Words Do You Say?

I love it when someone provides me with words of encouragement, it is so helpful to keep me going, to continue the project on which I am working. Don't you feel so much better when you receive words of encouragement? Do you get to hear encouragement often? I hope so.

How frequently are you the sender of positive, encouraging words? Let's hope daily; if not that often, then you may want to develop this as a new habit. Put reminder notes around so that you are more pro-active in saying positive things. In part of my training as a HeartMath Coach, I had to practice an Appreciation Day, a day to consciously express my appreciation at least 8 to 12 times. When I did this, I could see by the recipient's expression of delight or their simple smile, my comment touched them. So, I have made this a daily habit, to tell at least one person each day how much I appreciate them. It can be the cashier or bagger at the grocery store, the person at the car wash drying off my car, one of my children, and the list goes on. And one thing I added into my gratitude journal each day is whom I appreciated that day and if I have not yet done so, I get out of bed and send someone an email letting them know I appreciate them. If this resonates with you, you may want to develop this habit as well. If you do, let me know what impact it has on your life and those who receive it! Remember, what you give out comes back to you ten fold.

When you are being compassionate, you consider
another's situation with love rather than judgment.

Write down a list of people you would like to send or tell of your appreciation._____

_____

_____

_____

_____

_____

_____

_____

_____

_____

_____

_____

_____

_____

*"There is more hunger for love and appreciation in
this world than for bread."*
. . . Mother Teresa

Receiving Words Of Others . . .

I absolutely love it when someone pays me a compliment and I am sure that you do too. Doesn't it make your heart sing and you feel so full of love? WOW. Wouldn't it be wonderful to be in that state of emotion all the time? You would be happier and full of grace and joy at all times, which would definitely send out more harmonious energy in this world, thus creating a better world.

One thought that comes to mind about receiving compliments is this: how do you respond when someone gives you a compliment? I always find it interesting how people respond. Often they rebuff the compliment by responding in a somewhat negative manner. For instance, when someone tells you that you look good in a particular outfit, you respond, "Oh this old thing?" Or "Are you kidding me, I have had it for years." What kind of feeling is sent back to the bestower of the compliment? Do you think that it makes them feel good? Probably not. And if that happens very many times, they will be less likely to continue giving compliments to you.

We often try to make some excuse or explanation instead of just receiving the compliment. ("What, this old thing?" "My hair is such a mess, I am surprised you would even say that." And so on.) I am not sure how this has become such a standard response from people and I remember that there was a time in my life I did the same thing. Even though I cannot remember specifically when I became aware that when someone gives me a compliment all I really need to say is, "Thank you," I am glad that I no longer respond in a negative way. We don't need to justify anything about the "thing being complimented," just be willing to *receive* it. It then becomes a Win | Win for everyone.

When someone compliments you they are giving you a gift and it is up to you to receive the gift, or not. I think it is much harder to not receive a physical material gift than a verbal gift. Just relish in the gifts you are given.

"The greatest gift is a portion of thyself."
. . . Ralph Waldo Emerson

"Every gift from a friend is a wish for your happiness."
. . . Richard Bach

Part Five

Protective Chatter "Boundaries"

Negative Other Chatter . . .

How do you feel when the negative words flow out of someone toward you? We have all experienced that in our lives. Some people live that experience on a daily basis and think they do not have a choice to do otherwise. They do, you do. If you experience verbal abuse, you do have a choice, you may not like your choices, but think of yourself -- you don't have to live your life like this. This is not how we are meant to live our lives.

A couple of thoughts about why people use critical / negative words with others . . . There has been so much study about this and what I have found through years of reading and courses that I have taken, it comes right down to this: what others say to you is about them, it is a projection of their self-esteem, how they feel about about themselves; it is their "stuff." And remember, the reverse is true, how you react / respond to others is about how you are feeling about yourself. For instance, if you heard, "I can't believe you are so stupid." as a child, you probably started to question yourself, wondering if you are really stupid. Then you start to believe that you are stupid because your parent, sibling, bully or other adult told you that often, and since you learn from parents and other adults, then you naturally must believe them. As you grew, you continued to believe this and many other negative things about yourself. And as human nature would have it, you continue this by putting down others along your life journey. You will continue on this way until something changes and you become aware that this is not really who you want to be and that you are not stupid (or what other negative things people have said to you about you). At that point you make a choice, "I don't have to believe this any longer. It is not who I really am." And then you choose on a daily basis, maybe even hourly, to *not* believe that about yourself any longer. Once you make that choice, then you realize that you have a *choice to hear or not hear* what people want to say to you. You own your power.

Is it really that simple? Yes, it can be. It is often hard, yet worth every ounce of energy you put into it. There are various techniques that can make the journey a lot simpler. One way that I prefer is daily reading or listening to your affirmations, your "I am" statements. Remember, you did that at the beginning of the book where you wrote down the negative mind chatter and changed it to a positive, empowering statement.

(Author's note: there is a complimentary Affirmation Audio download available on my website: www.margaretmartin.com) When you really want to make changes such as treating others well, being respected, speaking and being spoken to with care, then you must make the commitment to write those down and commit to reading them daily as well as living your life that way – treating others the way you want to be treated. It really goes back to the Golden Rule: Do unto others as you would have them do unto you. You will be able to receive more of what you want when you walk your talk.

Learning about Boundaries

Once you make the choice to not put up with or tolerate the negativity of others, there are steps to take to protect yourself. Set boundaries. What is a boundary? A boundary is, just as it sounds, a protection line, invisible fence or bubble you imagine around you to protect you from the words and / or actions of others. Boundaries help you define who you are, your character, your values and who you are not. It is like a moat around a castle, to protect and establish a safe distance from other people's harm and negativity.

Here is how you do that. The steps are simple. First you determine that you must set a boundary. For instance, if there is someone with whom you regularly have phone conversations and in the beginning the conversation is pleasant or at least respectful, then the other person begins being negative to you or berating you or others about whom you care. They get on a tirade and before you know it you find yourself trying to defend yourself, but it doesn't do any good because they just keep on and on, and all that is being accomplished is they are spewing their stuff at you and you are either defending yourself or shrinking away within yourself beginning to believe all over again that what they are saying is true. This is when you realize that you must set a boundary. You have an "ah ha" moment, a moment when you realize they have crossed the line.

So again, determine what boundaries you want to set and realize with every boundary you set there is a consequence and a reaction to the boundary.

Then let people know that you will no longer find their behavior / words acceptable, advise them **not** to continue.

Steps to setting a Boundary:

Determine with whom you need to set a boundary and what it will be.

1) set the boundary and advise them
2) advise them they are crossing your boundary
3) warn them again and issue the consequences
4) take your action

Example: You are in a telephone conversation with someone and the conversation is going along well, when they change their tone and start criticizing you. Instead of reacting and defending yourself, at that point you set your boundary (1) "I just want to let you know that I am not going to be talked to like that by you or anyone else any more." Then (2) say, "You are talking to me in a manner that is unacceptable and if you continue (3) I will hang up the phone." Then if they continue (4) you would say, "I am hanging up the phone now." And do it! You hang up the phone. Should they call you back, you have the choice of answering the phone and saying, "Are you willing to talk to me in a manner that is more appropriate? If not, I will hang up again." Or don't answer the phone. A point to note: some people will go to great lengths to try to get to you. If they cannot reach you by phone, they may resort to email or letters. At least by email, you can block them and if letters come, you can choose not to read them or have someone else read them and tell you if there is anything of importance in them.

Throughout my life experience, I have had to set boundaries on many occasions. Here is one example that happened a few years ago when I was the project coordinator and president of my townhome community Board of Directors. Briefly, the community was experiencing renovations of our buildings; we had to establish that all the grounds within our community to be considered a "construction site" and there would be no playing on the grounds of the community except within a very small section, and that the children were to stay away from the construction trailer and all supplies. (Note, we had a community meeting that was for the children to meet with all of the professionals and the contractor involved so that they could have their questions answered and that the board of directors were being considerate of the children too in our project.) Needless to say, this was a problem, because the stacks of lumber and supplies were like a magnet to the kids, they wanted to play on them. When this happened, the parents were contacted and the situation was explained once again to them; I don't know if they didn't communicate the importance to their children or not, but it continued. More written reminders went out (as well as when we would see the children out there, reminding them nicely to play elsewhere). One dad called me and started yelling at me about the wording of the letters which had been formed by our attorney explaining the legal consequences as set forth by our insurance policies. I told him if he had concerns I would be happy to talk with him about it, but I would not be yelled at and talked to in that manner, and that if he continued I would hang up. He continued. So I told him, "I am hanging up now," which I did. Well, he called back and I let it go to voicemail.

The story actually goes on. After that happened a couple of times, he found my email address – searched the web, found my website and email address – and started sending me abusive emails, which I forwarded to the Board and the association attorney. After a few instances of this, the attorney mailed him a letter telling him that he could only communicate with me concerning the project and only in written communication that was placed in the box that was provided for the community members to communicate with the Board concerning the construction. This experience wasn't easy, it certainly wasn't fun, but had to be done. And as of this writing, this man and I are still living in the same community, we speak to each other when passing, and occasionally have a pleasant conversation

Consequences / Reaction

Be aware that you must be willing to put your needs and your self-care ahead of anyone else's needs and you must be willing to live with the consequences and their reaction to your stand. There are always some consequences, at least initially. Often people are hesitant to enforce their boundaries because they fear losing the friend, acquaintance, the business deal, opportunity, etc. Or he or she may be afraid of an overreaction or possible harm from the person with whom they are setting the boundary.

If you are hesitant to take this action you may be in avoidance or fear and you may already be suffering a huge consequence by not enforcing your boundary. This person is sucking the life out of you. They are controlling you. Is that what you want? If what you want is to be honored and respected, then do what it takes to take care of you.

****IMPORTANT****

Please Note: Do not put yourself in harm's way to set your boundaries. **Ask** for help from someone, an organization, domestic violence center, a counselor or attorney. This is what these people and organizations do. They are highly experienced and they can offer you support and guidance based on your specific needs. **My suggestions here are just that, suggestions. I do not offer legal or psychological counseling.**

In some cases, the hesitation to set boundaries is caused by living in an environment with someone who is not only verbally abusive, but physically abusive as well. If you are in this situation, please seek the help of your local domestic violence center as well as other professional help. It does take a lot of courage to make this choice, but know that *you are worth it* and you will be supported! Statistics show that the abuser will apologize and abuse again. There are people waiting to help you, many of whom have been through what you are going through and totally understand your situation, as best they can. Life is about living and living well! Make the choice today to take care of and honor yourself, and start living your life again.

Important - 2: if you are the one using critical words or behaviors against others, please seek assistance to change this behavior so that you can have more peace and joy in your life.

In my experience and the large amount of material I have read about verbally abusive people, they have often been raised in a similar type of environment and they do not know or haven't been yet able to learn a different way of communicating. Not only is it a habit, it is also control. Most abusers have been put down and beaten down one way or another their whole lives and often, that is all they know as well. Generally, they live in fear that they will lose control and if they lose control then they are vulnerable, and that is not a comfortable place for them to be.

The good news is that there are many sources and resources for help in making this very important change and usually, it is not as painful as you may think and from what I know from my own healing journey, it is such a freeing experience. Please see the resources section.

Important - 3: People will treat you as you allow them. So take good care of yourself, insist that all people treat you well.

This may sound counter intuitive, people treating us as we allow, but it really is the case. We grow up modeling behaviors of our parents and other role models, and rarely is there an example of someone advising you that you really are in charge of your life, to set standards to be treated well. Mostly you are given instruction to treat others well. If you take a moment and reflect on your early years, more than likely you will find that this is true. So you have the opportunity now to change things. Take responsibility for you, own your power and guide others as to how you would like to be treated. You can do this in small steps by gently telling a loved one to honor something that is important to you, such as: you want to have a few minutes to relax when you get home from work instead of charging into the kitchen and starting dinner; to really listen to you when you talk, to look you in the eyes so you know that you have their attention (and do the same for them), to speak to you in a nicer tone of voice. I am certain that you can think of many other examples.

> *"A loving relationship is one in which the loved one is free to be himself – to laugh with me, but never at me, to cry with me, but never because of me; to love life, to love himself, to love being loved. Such a relationship is based upon freedom and can never grow in a jealous heart."*
> *. . . Leo F. Buscaglia*

> *"Dripping water hollows out stone, not through force but through persistence."*
> *. . . Ovid*

> *"You and you alone choose moment by moment who and how you want to be in the world. . . . Own your power and show up for your life. Beam brighter."*
> *. . . Jill Bolte Taylor*

Part Six

USING WORDS of FUN

One of the greatest things in life is being with a friend or group of friends and sharing stories and laughing. There is little in life that makes you feel so good as to spend time laughing. The use of your words in fun and laughter generally creates such pleasure for those involved.

Many times it happens with long-time friends when they are gathered together and start sharing their stories, and life experiences. One story usually generates another and before you know it you have spent 30 minutes to several hours laughing. Laughing really generates positive energy and is often used in the healing process for the body.

Research:

Therapeutic Benefits of Laughter - www.holistichotline.com

Dr. Lee Berk and fellow researcher Dr. Stanley Tan of Loma Linda University in California have been studying the effects of laughter on the immune system. To date, their published studies have shown that laughing lowers blood pressure, reduces stress hormones, increases muscle flexion, and boosts immune function by raising levels of infection-fighting T-cells, disease-fighting proteins called Gamma-interferon and B-cells, which produce disease-destroying antibodies. Laughter also triggers the release of endorphins, the body's natural painkillers, and produces a general sense of well-being.

Laughter is Good for Your Heart, According to a University of Maryland Medical Center Study

Laughter, along with an active sense of humor, may help protect you against a heart attack, according to a new study by cardiologists at the University of Maryland Medical Center in Baltimore. The study, which is the first to indicate that laughter may help prevent heart disease, was presented at the American Heart Association's 73rd Scientific Sessions in New Orleans. The researchers found that people with heart disease were 40 percent less likely to laugh in a variety of situations compared to people of the same age without heart disease.

From the article **Laughter Benefits: the three C's,** *Learn the Many Benefits of Laughter to the Soul2*

"Laughter helps us cope when there is little else to cling to. It helps us see how utterly stupid we were to let the mole hill grow into Mt. Saint Helen's, about to pop its top. Laughter is the key ingredient to happy social gatherings, and is the marker for all of those great moments we remember. ("Remember the time...?") Laughter is helpful in large and small doses, but it is best when it is spontaneous. Let the scientists go on with their studies, and let the critics disdain the results; the rest of us will go on with life as we always have, doing the best with what we've got, thankful for the happiness and the laughter benefits that come with it."

Of course, I would recommend that this laughter be focused on positive experiences, not making fun of someone. That type of humor is sadistic and hurtful, thus creating negative energy for you and those involved. The idea is to use your words with fun and humor, it will lighten the atmosphere, and make you feel good which will increase your self-esteem and stimulate your brain.

I am sure that you have encountered people who are really funny. They have a natural wit, and aren't we thankful for them? They make life a joy. They also help us see many of the absurdities of life.

At a recent gathering of high school friends, we had a similar experience when one of our classmates kept us laughing so hard as she related many stories. I thanked her for making us laugh and her response was that she seemed to be able to make people laugh easily. What a gift! My friend said to me, "Life is funny and I just talk about life." Note – she has a very thick Southern accent which adds to the enjoyment of the stories.

Most everyone enjoys humor. Look at the success of the Comedy Central on television as well as the number of funny spots on YouTube. Think about how many times a week and in some cases, a day, that someone sends you a fun email. I sure enjoy getting them and I feel so much better after having received them and having a really good laugh. Some just create smiles while others are so funny I almost fall out of my chair! Now that would be funny too!

Spend more time laughing! It is good for your heart, your brain and your soul.

"There is nothing in the world so irresistibly contagious as laughter and good humor."
. . . Charles Dickens

"Always laugh when you can, it is cheap medicine."
. . . George Gordon Byron

Part Seven

More thoughts on The Chatter that Matters . . . .

INTEGRITY . . .

As you continue this journey of *The Chatter that Matters* . . . **Your Words ARE Your Power**, think about how you use your words to convey your integrity.

Webster's definition of integrity is:
1. Strict adherence to a standard of value or conduct
2. Personal honesty and independence
3. Completeness: unity
4. Soundness.

As you think about the meaning of this word that is so often used, how do you measure up? Are you a person of high integrity?

I began writing this during a year of campaigning for various political offices and have taken some time to reflect on the various people who have held that office over the last few years. You may have thought about this as well and questioned, "How well have they exemplified integrity?" And now as I look around to the people I know and notice that from time-to-time there is a conflict between what they do within their job and how they handle their personal life. In other words, they do an outstanding job in their work with what appears to be high integrity, yet in their personal life have very little integrity and try to keep it hidden from the public.

I do know people who are outstanding in their profession, considered the very BEST of their industry or profession, yet on a personal level, from my observation, they cannot keep the level of integrity high. You see them handling their business, their employees and their customers/clients/patients and you just couldn't ask for them to be more honest and perform to the highest standards, yet in their personal lives they don't. Some are verbally abusive to their children and spouse. Some have affairs while trying to convince their spouse and their friends that all is well. Some repeatedly make excuses for not showing up to see their children's activities when they have given their word to their children that they will be there. Some make excuses to families and friends about not showing up because of "this or that."

The truth is we often excuse these people, from politicians to our brother / sister / spouse, because they do a good job in their work. "They are helping the world." I don't know about you, but I wonder, what kind of impact does this really have? This is not an easy yes or no question. It is one that each of us will answer for ourselves.

I think if you just look around at society, you see the impact a lack of integrity has had all around us. Many people have become less interested in following through with their commitments, taking things that clearly are not theirs, taking advantage of others, putting others down so that they "look good," taking the easy way out of a difficult situation because they fear what others may say or think. Some make a commitment to show up and be responsible and productive at their jobs, yet do not. Well, the real truth of the matter is this; it can be difficult to trust these people. They are not authentic. In my experience, I have learned to cut people some slack for the fact that they, like I, are human and doing the best they can, but what about those people who are consistently exemplifying lack of integrity? I make a choice to do business with the people I know (as best I have the ability to know) have high integrity in their total lives, not just in one part. You can too.

Here is an example that comes to mind. I attended a multi-day workshop with an attendance of several hundred people. And as is the case of most all speakers and trainers, there is a courtesy that the attendees do not tape record the sessions and often there is a notification in the materials that the attendees are not allowed to tape the sessions. Well, about two or three days into this workshop the speaker looked down at one individual on the front row and asked what he is doing. The attendee responded that he was recording for his spouse who could not attend. Wow! I was blown away – as was the speaker. I could not believe that someone would have the audacity to do that, especially in a workshop where we had given a pledge to be there, show up on time, follow the guidelines and fully participate. The speaker handled it well by reminding the participant that taping was not allowed and if their spouse wanted to hear the program, then he could buy the cd's. He then went on with his presentation.

Now this individual claims to be an "expert" in a particular field and offers workshops and teleclasses. And as it happened, several months after this program, I was on a conference call with him and the purpose of the call was for this individual to help us with a particular focus area. By the time I got off the call, I felt worse than before. Most of the questions and responses by this person were extremely judgmental and demeaning of some members of our group who were not able to make the call and as it turned out, this individual just wanted to sell us on his workshop. This was the opposite of what he had indicated when he offered to provide some steps that would assist us. There was no real "meat" to the information he provided in the conference call, and it was what I call a "bait and switch." Our friend who had invited him was embarrassed and sent us an apology; he had let her down and disappointed her.

Do you, like I, want to work with and be around people who have similar standards and values to ours? Personally, I always try my very best to live up to my word, when I make a commitment I do all that I can to complete it. People can take me at my word. And just so you know, yes, every-now-and-then things happen that prevent me from fulfilling my commitment, but very rarely. Does that make me better than others? NO, it does not. That is a choice that I have made for me and if it resonates with you, you can too. Can we take you at your word? I think that this world could be a better place to live if we, individually, would make the effort to take pride in what we say and do.

Pride is a good thing even though often misused, misunderstood or misinterpreted. Again asking Webster; the definition of pride: *1. Proper respect for one's own dignity and worth; 2. Pleasure of satisfaction of something achieved, done or owned; 3. Excessive self-esteem or conceit.* So having pride about yourself is overall a really good thing, just try to stay away from the conceit part of pride! I especially like the first definition "proper respect for one's own dignity and worth," this is a great focus because it then helps you respect others more easily.

At this point, you may want to review what your standards and values are, choose to raise them and then set the example for your family, friends and colleagues. Expect more of yourself and others and let them know that you do. Do this only if you are willing to walk your talk; be willing not to ask more of others than you are of yourself. Just by doing this one thing, the quality of life of your neighborhood, your community, your state, your country and your world will improve. Yes, with just one person choosing to live in higher integrity our world improves.

Values

Values are: Activities, preferences or behaviors to which you are naturally drawn, who you are, what fulfills you. Something that is naturally important to you – whether it is beauty, creativity, family, honesty, or things of worth to you.

What values are not: Needs - resources, people, feelings, situations or environments you must have to be your best. Wants – what you enjoy having, provides gratification. Priorities – something you decide to do sooner than later.

Review the following list and circle those that are most important to you. Review all you have circled and choose the top 20. Note, this list is one that I have complied from several resources through my many years of coaching. You may want to add some additional words that may be appropriate for you.

Accepting

Acquiring

Adventuresome

Amused

Aroused

Assisting

Authentic

Awareness

Be connected

Be expert

Be in control

Be original

Be superior

Be the best

Be the greatest

Cause focused

Coach

Compassionate

Conceive ideas

Daring

Designer

Devoted

Discernment

Distinguishable

Educator

Embody excellence

Embody grace

Embody mastery

Empathize

Encourage

Enjoy beauty

Enjoy bliss

Enjoy elegance

Enlighten

Family focus

Feeler

Feel good

Flow with energy

Gambler

Glow

Have fun

Having taste

Honesty

Honoring

Imagination

Influence

Inspire

Integrity

Integrated

Judging

Kindness

Learner

Leader

Linked

Love

Loveable

Nurturer

Observer

Outdo

Passionate

Perceiver

Persuader

Planner

Provider

Relater

Relate w/Spirit

Respond

Risk

Rule

Sensitive

Serve

Set standards

Spark

Spiritual

Stimulate

Strength / Strong

Tender

The unknown

Thrill

Thoughtful

To improve

Triumph

Trusting

Trustworthy

Uplift

Win over

The difference between needs, wants and values:

- A need is something you *must* have in order to be your best, such as time, space, money love and such. Usually, getting a need met causes you to feel satisfaction.
- A want is something that you relate to by trying to acquire or experience it. Usually, getting something you want makes you feel gratification.
- A value is something that you naturally gravitate toward, prompted from within and not by needs or want.

Distinctions: If there is urgency, it is probably a need. If there is a craving or desire, it is probably a want. If there is a natural and uncomplicated pull, it's probably a value. Being able to distinguish among all three takes a little practice, but one of the many benefits is that you will understand yourself better and make better decisions, because decisions based on your core values will have more chance of being right and staying right for a long time. Decisions based on wants and needs are not as likely to be beneficial on a continuous basis.

Look back at the exercise above. Now prune your 20 values down to five.

Margaret Martin

List them here:

1. _____

   _____

   _____

2. _____

   _____

   _____

3. _____

   _____

   _____

4. _____

   _____

   _____

5. _____

   _____

   _____

These are your core values.

> *"You must take personal responsibility. You cannot change the circumstances, the seasons, or the win, but you can change yourself."*
> *. . . Jim Rohn*

RESPONSIBILITY

As history shows throughout time, agreements and contracts have been around, they were sealed with the parties giving their word that the agreement would be done and at some time a handshake was added or their seal on the document. We have evolved to a point that for legal contracts to be binding, a simple agreement and handshake is rarely valid any longer. Is that because there is no recourse? In "olden times," simple humiliation (by making the individual stand in front of the entire town and the official read to everyone what the individual had/had not done and sometimes they were thrown out of the town) was really all that was needed to enact compliance. Some cultures go as far as cutting off a finger or even a hand. Today, when buying a home that has a mortgage, you must sign what seems to be 40 - 50 pages, then witnessed and notarized. Other contracts have many, many pages all of which almost take the fun out of any "deal" and written in "legalese" that hardly anyone of us who are not in the legal profession would understand. But on the bright side, it protects all parties involved.

Let's take a look at what being responsible really means. Webster says:

1. Having to account for one's actions: answerable
2. Having a duty or an obligation
3. Being a source or a cause
4. Dependable

So how is it you are responsible? How does it fit for you? And how does this relate to *The Chatter that Matters*? Word given = Responsibility. I can think of a few ways, such as when you become a parent, you are responsible for that child in so many ways: their food, their care, loving them, giving them guidance and so on. Then another way of being responsible is having a job and having the duty or obligation to show up at the arranged times to produce the work to which you have agreed. Yet another, doing what you say, whether it is verbal or written, you will do: showing up for an appointment on time, doing what you agreed to do for an organization. There are many other examples, can you think of any? If so, you may want to write them here:

_____

_____

_____

_____

_____

_____

_____

_____

_____

_____

When you are responsible, it communicates that you are dependable, you are honest and trustworthy. It communicates your level of integrity. It says everything about who you are and what your values are.

Every day you have the choice to show up and do the stuff you have said that you will do. Honor your commitments. Sometimes to be really responsible you have to push to make sure that things get done by the deadline to which you have committed. Often there are consequences if you do not. The consequences might not be really big, but any time you do not meet your deadline or show up when you said that you would; you may not be aware but, it erodes your self-esteem. That often triggers negative self-talk – *Negative Mind Chatter* – or *Chatter Splatter* - which we have previously discussed. When you do complete your responsibility, you feel really great, relieved, or just complete. What else happens when you are responsible? It does remind and confirm to people that they can count on you; you can be trusted and that will increase your self-esteem, and you will feel better about yourself!

Now let's look at a few examples how responsibility can be misused.

1) You give your word that you will do something for someone else and then you don't, with or without any valid reason. Will they be as likely to trust you again? Most of us will give people second and third chances, which is fair, but how long will you tolerate irresponsibility? How long will you allow people to treat you badly? The answer of course, is up to you.

2) What happens when people sign an agreement to follow rules or guidelines of the organization and then don't follow through, or abide by the rules consistently? Who do they hurt and does it make a difference? On a large scale it might not make a huge difference, but one thing to remember here is that it will have an impact on others and that impact can often be huge. Every circumstance is different and there are many legal ramifications that can be imposed as well. (This is certainly not my area of expertise).

Another consideration is that you, individually, will have less trust in that person whether you are directly impacted or not. Being an observer to situations such as this will cause you to form an opinion of the "perpetrator," thus determining your perspective level of integrity. And should the time come when you get to work with them on a committee or job of some variety, you will remember the previous situation and probably wonder if that will have a negative impact on their performance on this project. It is a red flag to their integrity!

3) A very simple example is one of not showing up on time. This example is all around, just observe how often people consistently arrive on time for functions and how many constantly show up late?

One question to ask the consistent latecomers that comes to mind is, "What was more important in your life than letting me know that you would be late?" That is a bold approach which can be softened, the point being to the latecomer about the possible damage that can happen by their being late. This was brought up when we talked about responsibility so I won't repeat it here. That is a huge breech of responsibility.

One quick reminder here is, yes, life happens and there are exceptions. The key word here is: *consistently*. After reading the examples, do any incidents come to mind that remind you of a time when you have not been responsible? I know there have been a few (or maybe more) times that I haven't and I was reminded the hard way that people count on me to do what I have said that I will do.

List 3 examples of irresponsibility, yours or others:

1. _____
   _____
   _____
   _____

2. _____
   _____
   _____
   _____

3. _____
   _____
   _____
   _____

So perhaps the simplest way to explain is this: when you are being responsible, you do what you commit to doing, when you are not you will blame someone else for the situation, or you will shame yourself for not having followed through or justify all the reasons why you didn't. It really is just that simple, either you show up or you don't, and if people want to know why you didn't they will ask - for the most part, they don't really care about the "why you didn't"!

What are some of the ways you can improve your level of integrity and responsibility, it is worth the commitment to do so.

List them here:

_____

_____

_____

_____

_____

_____

Part Eight
PUTTING IT TOGETHER

Let's put this all together; it is really very simple, though not necessarily easy.

1. Be the person you want to be, the person you tell others that you are. Be true to yourself.

> *"What lies before us and what lies
> behind us are small matters compared
> to what lies within us."*
> *. . . Henry David Thoreau*

> *"To thine ownself be true and you
> will be false to no man."*
>
> *. . . Shakespeare*

2. Be open and honest with others. You may be amazed at what a positive impact on the lives of others you will have by doing just that one thing.

> *"Keep true, never be ashamed of
> doing right. Decide onwhat you think is
> right, and stick to it."*
> *. . . George Elliot*

3. Seek and speak the truth. When you don't it will catch up with you eventually, but you probably already know that.

> *"Character is what you have*
> *when nobody is looking."*
> .... *Marie Dresslar*

4. Speak from your heart to others and especially to yourself.

> *"A man is what he thinks about all day long."*
> ... *Ralph Waldo Emerson*

5. Set boundaries to protect yourself from the negativity of others.

> *"You teach other people how*
> *to treat you whether you are*
> *aware of it or not."*
> ... *Anonymous*

6. Take full responsibility for your actions. No blaming others, shaming yourself, or justifying your actions or lack of actions.

> *"You must take personal responsibility.*
> *You cannot change the circumstances,*
> *the seasons, or the wind, but you*
> *can change yourself."*
> ... *Jim Rohn.*

7.   Review your values; know what is really important to you.

> *"Act with courage and dignity;*
> *stick to the ideals that give meaning to life."*
> *. . . J. Nehru, Prime Minister of India*

8.   Don't make assumptions of others. Remember the saying, that to know someone, you must walk a mile in their shoes. And to do that, you must first take your shoes off.

> *"There is neither good nor bad,*
> *but thinking makes it so."*
> *. . . Shakespeare*

9.   Do the best you can under all circumstances. Most of us are way too hard on ourselves when we've not lived up to our own expectations; we usually beat ourselves up for it. If you always do your best, then there will be no beating up to be done!

> *"There is no failure except*
> *in no longer trying."*
> *. . . Elbert Hubbard*

10. Most of all, Love yourself. Be kind and gentle to YOU.

> *"I remember to love myself first and foremost.*
> *If I don't love myself, no one else will. "*
> *. . . Anonymous*

Resources

Jack Canfield
The Jack Canfield Companies
PO Box 30880, Santa Barbara, CA 93130
800-237-8336
www.jackcanfield.com
Workshop: Breakthrough to Success

Masaru Emoto
1F Eastside Bldg, Yanagibashi
Taito-ku, Tokyo, Japan 111-0052
+81-33863-0216
www.masaru-emoto.net
Water Experiment

Louise Hay
Hay House, Inc.
PO Box 5100,   Carlsbad, CA 92018
800-654-5123
www.hayhouse.com
Book: *You Can Heal Your Life*, Hay House, Inc.

Lauren McLaughlin
Unity Now
Clearwater, FL
727-531-8516
www.unitynow.com
Book: *Go to ELF*

Afterword

Now that you have finished processing the journey through *The Chatter that Matters* . . . **Your Words ARE Your Power**, your journey has really only begun. I am grateful that you have taken the time, effort and energy to read and it is my hope that you will return to this book from time-to-time to read and process again and again. As you continue your life journey you learn more and more each day and I think it is valuable to process books such as this about once a year. It helps you see your growth.

It is my understanding that we are meant to live a life filled with joy, to be at peace and to have fulfillment in our time here and it is through books such as this that helps clear the path, clear out the clutter of old ways of using your words, of allowing people to treat as they want. To change, grow and own your power by teaching those around you to treat you – in their words and actions – the way you want to be treated is ultimately up to you, there is no one else to blame. Is it challenging and scary sometimes; you bet and you will find that it is worth it. YOU are worth it.

Make sure as you start this process that you have a support system, it will be most helpful. Your support system can be friends, a particular support group, a MasterMind group (more information in the Resources section) or a Coach. By having the support system you will be able to stay on target with your goal of improvement and change, they will be there to provide the encouragement and keep you focused on your desired outcome.

Enjoy your journey.

Other resources:

National Domestic Violence Hotline
800-799-SAFE (7233) 24 hours a day, 7 days a week
www.thehotline.org
www.ndvh.org

Mastermind Groups
Free download at http://www.margaretmartin.com/products.html

The Purpose of a MaterMind Group

Every winning athlete and successful business person has a team of experts behind them. How would you like a team of hand-picked advisors committed to your personal success? What could you do with expert advice, wise counsel, and a network of successful people at your finger-tips?

The concept of a MasterMind Group was first introduced in Napoleon Hill's book, *Think and Grow Rich,* where he had interviewed all the people of the day who were extremely successful – a project requested by Andrew Carnegie. The concept is clearly explained below, and it is still worthy advice for any budding entrepreneur and anyone desiring success in their work and personal life:

(a) Ally yourself with a group of six to eight people for the creation and carrying out of your plan or plans for the accumulation of making use of the "MasterMind" principle

(b) Before forming your MasterMind alliance, decide what advantages and benefits you may offer the individual members of your group, in return for their cooperation. No one will work indefinitely without some form of compensation. No intelligent person will either request or expect another to work without adequate compensation, although this may not always be in the form of money.

(c). Arrange to meet with the members of your MasterMind group at least twice a week, and more often if possible, until you have jointly perfected the necessary plans or plans for the accumulation of money.

(d) Maintain perfect harmony between yourself and every member of your MasterMind group. If you fail to carry out this instruction to the letter, you may expect to meet with failure. The MasterMind principle cannot obtain where perfect harmony does not prevail.

Keep in mind these facts:

FIRST: you are engaged in an undertaking of major importance to you. To be sure of success, you must have plans which are faultless

SECOND: you must have the advantage of the experience, education, native ability and imagination of other minds as well as confidentiality to share any and all concerns. This is in harmony with the methods followed by every person who has accumulated a great fortune.

There is synergy of energy, commitment, and excitement that participants bring to a MasterMind Group. The beauty of MasterMind Groups is that participants raise the bar by challenging each other to create and implement goals, brainstorm ideas, and support each other with total honesty, respect and compassion. MasterMind participants act as catalysts for growth, devil's advocates and supportive colleagues.

The concept of the MasterMind Group was formally introduced by Napoleon Hill in the early 1900's. In his timeless classic, "Think And Grow Rich" he wrote about the MasterMind principle as:

"The coordination of knowledge and effort of two or more people, who work toward a definite purpose, in the spirit of harmony."

He continues...

"No two minds ever come together without thereby creating a third, invisible intangible force, which may be likened to a third mind."

In a MasterMind group, the agenda belongs to the group, and each person's participation is key. Your peers give you feedback, help you brainstorm new possibilities, and set up accountability structures that keep you focused and on track. You will create a community of supportive colleagues who will brainstorm together to move the group to new heights.

You'll gain tremendous insights, which can improve your business and personal life. Your MasterMind Group is like having an objective board of directors.

What Will You Get From It?
- Experience, skill and confidence
- Accountability and real progress in your business and personal life
- An instant and valuable support network
- A sense of shared endeavor - there are others out there!
- Design things to be the way you want them to be, not as you've been told they "should" be

Conducting a MasterMind Meeting:

The best size of a group is 5 – 6 people. If it is too much smaller it loses its dynamics, too much bigger, gets unwieldy.

Ideally, each MasterMind meeting should be conducted weekly or every other week, for one to two hours, in person. Many groups are successful via Skype or phone as well. Each meeting should follow the format suggested below – it works.

The facilitator and timekeeper roles need to rotate through the group so that all have an opportunity to participate. Someone will volunteer to be the facilitator and another to be the timekeeper for the next meeting at the end of each meeting or the rotation can be put on a calendar several months in advance. This assures that the meeting stays on track and all get a chance to participate and get feedback.

It is recommended in the first few meetings each person gets at least 30 minutes (rotating around the group) to familiarize the others to their situation, needs, and challenges – while other members brainstorm ways they can support that individual.

Guidelines:

1. Invocation – Ask for Spiritual Guidance
   MasterMind meetings should start with a request for the group to be filled and surrounded with powerful spiritual energy. Members can rotate to provide the invocation – using whatever spiritual belief structure the reader has, asking for spiritual energy to assist the group with each other's needs.

2. Share –
   What is New and Good / What you have learned since the last meeting
   This is a good way to keep the energy and excitement high and further bond with each other. Small successes are important. – 1 minute per person. It is important to be laser focused and timely.

3. Negotiate for Time -
   The usual time allotted to each person may be 10 minutes, there may be times when someone needs extra time to discuss

a particularly challenging situation. During this part, that individual will request an additional amount of time – be specific. Usually someone will give up a portion of their time – the timekeeper makes note of who it is and how much time is donated which will be reduced from the donator's time to share. Or if there are several challenging situations the group may decide to extend that day's session if possible.

It is the job of the Timekeeper to be diligent about keeping members on track. Everyone deserves equal time and equal guidance and the Timekeeper will insure this.

4. Sharing Time –
    Individuals Speak while the Group listens and brainstorms solutions - What kind of discussions can you expect during a MasterMind meeting? "I need contacts. I need referrals. I am at a loss at this new aspect of my business. I am looking for expert to help me develop this idea." These are just some of the things that might come up.

    Note: sometimes it may take a while to explain your situation, so you may want to devote the last 2 – 5 minutes of the individual sharing time for brainstorming.

    Discussions can be personal or professional – it doesn't matter. As long as everyone is getting value, they will stay involved with the group. As long as you are giving value, everyone will want to be there. All information shared in a MasterMind group is confidential – a must to be agreed upon by all.

    During this part, the Timekeeper will give a 2 minute (or whatever time is decided for brainstorming) warning, then

30 second warning so that they can wrap-up their time. The Timekeeper then advises the segment has ended.

5. Make a Commitment to Stretch -
    Once all members have had their time to share, discuss, brainstorm, give feedback, the Timekeeper goes around the group and asks for commitments to be accomplished by the next meeting. It needs to be a stretch. I suggest everyone write down their commitments so that they can report the upcoming meeting as to whether they have been successful.

    Making commitments insures that everyone is moving forward and has support of the group when needed.

6. End with Gratitude -
    You can end your session with a prayer expressing gratitude. Or you might go around the table allowing each member to say one thing they appreciate from the meeting.

7. Be Accountable -
    When members assemble at the next meeting, each member needs to share something related to the goal (commitment) they set at the previous meeting. Did each member take action? Did they achieve their goal?

8. Consequences -
    To help with accountability and stretching your commitments, it is a good idea to set-up consequences for commitments not achieved. Some groups will decide on an additional donation to charity, over and above their usual amount, such as $25 or even $100. Others have added to that donation a requirement of the individual getting up at 3:00am to have a "Walk with God" to

explain what was more important in their lives than getting the action completed.

You may also want to download this from my website: www. MargaretMartin.com, just go to the products page where you will find it listed as a free download.

If you are interested in joining a group that is hosted by an experienced facilitator, contact Charlyn Shelton, MasterMind Mentor, www.CharlynShelton.com, 321-446-5334.

Acknowledgements

To My children, Bill Strupp, Meg Strupp Lokey, and David Strupp and their spouses, Kerri Davis Strupp and Michael Lokey, you provided me with the courage to go forward and tell my story so that our experiences can help others. You are always an advocate for me in all that I do and trust that somehow it will always work out for the best in the long run. You can't imagine how thrilled that I am that all of you provide such wonderful support and encouragement for each other, and for that I am very blessed and very grateful. I am so proud of each one of you.

To my sister, Helen Martin Keaton, I love you dearly and greatly appreciate your love, friendship, encouragement and support throughout my life. I would be lost without you. And to John Keaton, the best brother-in-law anyone could ever ask for – your constant love, support and sense of humor keep me going.

To my dear parents, Milton and Mary Elizabeth Martin, who watch over me from heaven, thank you for all the gifts you have given me and your constant encouragement and support from the other side, I am so grateful to have chosen you. Mother, you left this earth too soon for me to know you well, yet the legacy you left to me is beautiful. Daddy, I know you are with me always – thank you.

To my cousin, Ann Belew McCafferty, who is now watching over me from heaven as well – you have always been my greatest support, my biggest cheerleader and a terrific sounding board for me in the rough times. I thank you and I miss you.

My best friend in the whole world, Barbara Stein, has been more of a support than she will ever know. We have been though "thick and thin" and managed to stay sane somehow, perhaps because of our sense of humor and dedication to each other. Your love, friendship and constant support is a gift for which there is no monetary value.

To the ladies of the Sacred Circle – Charlyn Shelton, Lauren McLaughlin, Janet Connor, Susan Miner, Celeste Thomas and Margo Mastromarchi – thank you for the visioning, encouragement and believing in me to complete this project. You earth angels help so many and I am grateful to be a part of such a spiritually powerful group of women. Charlyn, you have been on this "book journey" since it was birthed in 2007, I love you and thank you for always keeping me looking forward at the possibilities.

My friend and now colleague, Peggy Rometo – Intuitive Healer and author of, The Little Book of Big Promises, thank you for helping me get back in touch with my deep spiritual roots. Through your guidance, confidence and love, you have helped me embrace that I am a healer, a lightworker – which still surprises me most days.

To my friend Rayme Nuckels, thank you for providing me with numerous opportunities to tell the story of The Chatter that Matters in the form of keynote presentations to various organizations. I am grateful for your friendship and your belief in me and my work.

I am grateful to my two editors, Denise McCabe and Allison Loy, who helped me make better sense with my writing, corrected my grammar and who confirmed that this book was worthy of being published. Thank you for your encouragement.

And to my twelfth grade English teacher, Mrs. Majorie Woodell, it was your teaching early in my life that has helped me to remember all that you taught – well, except for the diagramming of sentences – and to make this project easier for my editors and publishers. I appreciate your encouragement last year in 2011 as I told you I was writing a book – you didn't seem surprised and that amazed me.

To the many people at Balboa Press, thank you for your guidance as I learned about the self-publishing process. Thank you for putting your expert touches on my book to make it beautiful.

There are many other people to whom I am grateful for their trust, friendship and belief in my work; too numerous to list here. You are the people who attend my workshops, keynotes, read my blog and newsletter and stay connected to me via social media – thank you.

As we continue the journey of this life together, thank you for your companionship along the way. And remember always . . . it's the Chatter that Matters.

Much love and gratitude to you all,

Namaste,

Margaret

End Notes:

1 - **Laughter Is Good For Your Heart, According To A New University Of Maryland Medical Center Study -- from:** http://www.umm.edu/news/releases/laughter.htm
Contact: Barbara Crawford, bcrawfor@umm.edu, 410-328-8919

2 - **Laughter Benefits: the three C's,** *Learn the Many Benefits Of Laughter To The Soul*
By E. E. Kane LifeScript www.lifescript.com

About the Author

Margaret Martin has been on a life long journey of personal and professional development. In this guidebook she pulls together some of the most impactful yet easy to use processes to help you keep your life focused on the positive. Her mission is to help people make a positive difference in their own lives so that they can experience a meaningful life of peace ~ joy ~ fulfillment. She is your *Means to Positive Change.*

As a Speaker | Coach | Author | Facilitator, Margaret has been providing her clients and followers the gift of helping them look at their life situations from a different perspective for over 20 years.

She lives in Clearwater, FL where continues her work based on The Chatter that Matters, and maintains her "Priority 'ONE' – Taking You to the Top of Your List - coaching practice. Active in her community through various organizations and Margaret also provides coaching to MBA students at the University of Tampa. Known for her hospitality and love of entertaining, you wouldn't be surprised to find her house filled with family and friends.

You may reach Margaret:

PO Box 14603, Clearwater, FL 33766

727-725-3370

Website: www.MargaretMartin.com

www.TheChatterthatMatters.com

Blog: www.MargaretsNotes.com

Social Media:

Twitter: www.twitter.com/MargaretMartin

Facebook: www.facebook.com/MargaretMartin.SpeakerCoach

LinkedIn: http://www.linkedin.com/MargaretMartin

~ Notes ~

~ Notes ~

~ Notes ~

~ Notes ~

~ Notes ~

~ *Notes* ~

~ Notes ~

~ Notes ~